I0505243

Table Of Contents

Introduction

What is network marketing and MLM?

What is Network Marketing and MLM?

Network marketing and MLM (multi-level marketing) are two terms that are often used interchangeably. But what do they really mean? Simply put, network marketing is a business model that involves recruiting a network of people to sell a company's products or services. MLM is a specific type of network marketing where distributors earn commissions not only on their own sales, but also on the sales of the people they recruit into the network.

Network marketing has been around for over 70 years, but it has gained popularity in recent years due to the rise of social media and the internet. It is a business model that allows people to start their own business without any significant upfront investment. Instead, they can earn commissions on the sales they make and the sales made by their team.

MLM is a more complex form of network marketing, where distributors earn commissions on multiple levels of their network. This means that when someone they recruit makes a sale, they earn a commission not only on that sale but also on the sales made by the people that person recruits. This creates a pyramid-shaped structure where the top earners are those who have recruited the most people and built the largest network.

Both network marketing and MLM are legitimate business models that have produced many successful entrepreneurs. However, they have also been associated with scams and pyramid schemes, which have given them a bad reputation. It is important to research any company before joining and to be cautious of any opportunity that promises quick riches without any effort.

In order to be successful in network marketing and MLM, it is important to have a strong work ethic, excellent communication skills, and a willingness to learn and grow. It is also important to choose a company and product that you believe in and are passionate about. With hard work and dedication, it is possible to earn a significant income through network marketing and MLM.

Why network marketing and MLM?

The idea of earning a passive income that can replace your full-time job is a dream for many people. However, the question remains, "how can I achieve this?" One answer is through network marketing and MLM. In this subchapter, we will discuss why network marketing and MLM are excellent opportunities for anyone who wants to earn a significant amount of money.

Firstly, network marketing and MLM offer a low barrier to entry. Unlike traditional businesses that require a significant amount of capital to start, network marketing and MLM only require a small investment to get started. This means that anyone can start a network marketing or MLM business, regardless of their financial situation.

Secondly, network marketing and MLM offer a flexible schedule. Most people have a busy schedule, and finding the time to start a business can be challenging. However, network marketing and MLM allow you to work at your own pace, and you can work from anywhere in the world. This means that you can work your business around your existing commitments, making it an excellent opportunity for busy individuals.

Thirdly, network marketing and MLM offer an opportunity to build a passive income. Unlike traditional jobs where you are paid for the hours you work, network marketing and MLM offer the opportunity to build a team of individuals who will work for you. This means that you can earn a passive income from the efforts of others, allowing you to earn money even when you are not working.

Fourthly, network marketing and MLM offer an opportunity to build valuable skills. To be successful in network marketing and MLM, you need to develop skills such as leadership, communication, and marketing. These skills are valuable in any industry, and developing them through network marketing and MLM can benefit you in your career or other businesses.

In conclusion, network marketing and MLM offer a low barrier to entry, a flexible schedule, an opportunity to build a passive income, and an opportunity to develop valuable skills. These benefits make network marketing and MLM an excellent opportunity for anyone who wants to earn a significant amount of money.

Who can benefit from network marketing and MLM?

Who Can Benefit from Network Marketing and MLM?

Network marketing and MLM are not only for those who are looking for a full-time job or those who want to earn some extra money. It is a business opportunity that can benefit anyone who is willing to put in the effort and dedication required to succeed.

Adults who are looking for financial freedom can benefit from network marketing and MLM. This business model provides an opportunity to earn a significant amount of money without having to work long hours or have extensive experience. It is an excellent way to supplement one's income or even replace their current job.

Business owners can also benefit from network marketing and MLM. By incorporating it into their existing business, they can expand their customer base and generate more income. Network marketing and MLM can also help businesses build a strong brand and create loyal customers.

Parents who want to spend more time with their families can benefit from network marketing and MLM. It provides them with the flexibility to work from home and choose their own schedule. This business model allows parents to earn a substantial income while also being present for their children.

Employees who are looking for a way to earn more money can benefit from network marketing and MLM. It provides them with an opportunity to earn extra income without having to work overtime or take on a second job. Network marketing and MLM can also help employees develop new skills and improve their communication and leadership skills.

Employers who want to provide their employees with an additional income stream can benefit from network marketing and MLM. By offering it as a side hustle, employers can help their employees earn extra income and improve their financial situation.

Self-employed individuals can also benefit from network marketing and MLM. It provides them with an additional income stream that can help them grow their business and improve their financial situation.

Networkers and marketers can benefit from network marketing and MLM by expanding their network and reaching new customers. It provides them with an opportunity to earn more money and improve their communication and leadership skills.

Marketing managers can benefit from network marketing and MLM by incorporating it into their marketing strategy. It provides them with an additional channel to reach new customers and generate more revenue.

Entertainers who are looking for additional income streams can benefit from network marketing and MLM. It provides them with an opportunity to earn money while also engaging with their fans and building a strong community.

Start-ups who are looking for innovative ways to generate revenue can benefit from network marketing and MLM. It provides them with a proven business model that can help them grow their business and reach new customers.

Retired individuals who are looking for a way to supplement their retirement income can benefit from network marketing and MLM. It provides them with an opportunity to earn money while also staying active and engaged in their community.

In conclusion, network marketing and MLM are not limited to a specific group of people. Anyone who is willing to put in the effort and dedication required to succeed can benefit from this business opportunity. It provides individuals with the flexibility to work from home, earn extra income, and improve their financial situation.

What this book will cover

This book, From Zero to $10,000 Monthly: Your Ultimate Network Marketing and MLM Blueprint, is a comprehensive guide that covers everything you need to know about network marketing and MLM. It is designed to be a valuable resource for adults, business owners, parents, employees, employers, self-employed individuals, networkers, marketers, marketing managers, entertainers, start-ups, and retirees who are interested in learning how to earn $10,000 per month through network marketing and MLM.

The book is divided into several chapters, each of which covers a specific topic related to network marketing and MLM. The first chapter provides an introduction to the world of network marketing and MLM, including the history of the industry, how it works, and the benefits of being involved in it.

The second chapter focuses on the importance of setting goals in network marketing and MLM. It provides practical tips on how to set realistic and achievable goals, and how to stay motivated and focused on achieving them.

The third chapter covers the essential skills needed to succeed in network marketing and MLM, including communication, leadership, and sales. It provides practical advice on how to develop these skills and how to apply them in your network marketing and MLM business.

The fourth chapter is all about building your network marketing and MLM business. It provides practical tips on how to find and recruit new prospects, how to build relationships with them, and how to train and motivate your team.

The fifth chapter covers the various marketing strategies that you can use to promote your network marketing and MLM business. It includes both offline and online marketing strategies, such as social media marketing, email marketing, and content marketing.

The sixth chapter focuses on the importance of personal branding in network marketing and MLM. It provides practical tips on how to develop your personal brand, how to promote it, and how to leverage it to build your network marketing and MLM business.

The seventh chapter covers the legal and ethical considerations of network marketing and MLM. It provides an overview of the laws and regulations that govern the industry, and offers practical advice on how to conduct your business in an ethical and compliant manner.

Overall, this book is a must-read for anyone who wants to learn how to earn $10,000 per month through network marketing and MLM. It is packed with practical advice, real-life examples, and valuable resources that will help you achieve your goals and build a successful network marketing and MLM business.

The Basics of Network Marketing and MLM

How network marketing and MLM work

Network marketing and MLM, or multi-level marketing, are two terms that are often used interchangeably. However, they are two different marketing strategies with a similar structure.

Network marketing is a business model where individuals or independent distributors promote and sell products or services directly to consumers. They earn a commission on the sales they make and also on the sales made by the team they recruit.

MLM, on the other hand, is a marketing strategy that allows individuals to earn money not only from their sales but also from the sales made by the people they have recruited. The structure of an MLM company is usually in the form of a pyramid, where the people at the top earn the most commissions.

Both network marketing and MLM rely heavily on building relationships with potential customers and team members. It is essential to establish trust and credibility with your audience to succeed in this industry.

To earn $10,000 per month through network marketing and MLM, you must have a solid understanding of the products or services you are promoting. You must also be able to effectively communicate the benefits of these products or services to potential customers.

Building a strong team is also crucial to your success. You must be able to recruit and train individuals who share your passion and vision for the business.

Another essential factor in succeeding in network marketing and MLM is consistency. You must be willing to put in the time and effort to grow your business and never give up, even when faced with challenges.

In conclusion, network marketing and MLM are viable business models that offer individuals the opportunity to earn a significant income. However, success in this industry requires a combination of knowledge, skills, and hard work. By following the right strategies and building a strong team, you can achieve your financial goals and create a successful network marketing or MLM business.

Understanding the compensation plan

Understanding the compensation plan is crucial to success in network marketing and MLM. It is the system by which you will be rewarded for your efforts and achievements in building your business. While every company has its own unique compensation plan, there are some common elements that you should understand.

First, there are usually two main ways to earn income in network marketing and MLM: through retail sales and through building a team. Retail sales involve selling the company's products or services directly to customers. Building a team involves recruiting and training other people to also sell the products or services, and earning a percentage of their sales.

Second, most compensation plans include various ranks or levels that you can achieve as you build your business. These ranks are often based on the volume of sales generated by you and your team, and typically come with increased bonuses and commissions.

Third, there are usually several types of bonuses and commissions that you can earn, such as fast start bonuses, leadership bonuses, and residual income. Fast start bonuses are paid when you enroll a new team member who makes a qualifying purchase. Leadership bonuses are paid when you reach higher ranks in the company and have a certain number of people in your downline. Residual income is paid on a recurring basis for as long as your team members continue to make sales.

It's important to note that while the compensation plan lays out the potential rewards for your efforts, it is not a guarantee of income. Your success will depend on your own hard work, dedication, and ability to effectively market and sell the products or services.

In order to maximize your earnings, it's essential to familiarize yourself with your company's compensation plan and set realistic goals for your business. Focus on building a strong team and providing excellent customer service, and you'll be on your way to earning $10,000 per month through network marketing and MLM.

Choosing the right company

Choosing the right company is crucial if you want to succeed in network marketing and MLM. With so many companies out there, it can be overwhelming to choose the right one. However, if you take the time to do your research, you can find a company that aligns with your values, interests, and goals.

The first thing you should consider when choosing a company is the products or services they offer. It's important that you believe in and use the products or services yourself. If you don't believe in what you're selling, it will be difficult to convince others to buy them. Moreover, reputable companies offer high-quality products or services that meet a genuine need in the market.

Another crucial factor to consider is the compensation plan. Make sure you understand how the company pays its distributors and whether the compensation plan is sustainable. A good compensation plan should reward distributors for their hard work and provide incentives for them to grow their business.

It's also important to research the company's history and reputation. Look for a company that has been around for at least a few years and has a proven track record of success. Check for any lawsuits or controversies that the company may have faced in the past. A reputable company should be transparent about their business practices and should have a positive reputation in the industry.

Finally, consider the support and training that the company offers its distributors. A good company should provide training and support to help you succeed in your business. Look for a company that offers regular training sessions, online resources, and a supportive community of distributors.

In conclusion, choosing the right company is essential if you want to succeed in network marketing and MLM. Take the time to research different companies, consider their products and compensation plan, and evaluate their reputation and support. By choosing the right company, you can build a successful business and achieve your financial goals.

Creating a successful mindset

Creating A Successful Mindset

Success is more than just achieving goals and accumulating wealth. It starts with having the right mindset. A successful mindset is a combination of positive thinking, resilience, and determination. It is the foundation for achieving success in any field, including network marketing and MLM.

Here are some tips to help you develop a successful mindset:

1. Believe in yourself
The first step to creating a successful mindset is to believe in yourself. You must have faith in your abilities and trust that you can achieve success. Cultivate a positive attitude and surround yourself with people who will encourage and support you.

2. Set realistic goals

Setting goals is essential to achieving success. However, it is important to set realistic goals that are achievable. When setting goals, consider your strengths and weaknesses, and be specific about what you want to achieve. Write down your goals and keep them visible as a daily reminder of what you are working towards.

3. Develop a growth mindset

A growth mindset is the belief that you can improve and develop your skills and abilities with hard work and dedication. It is essential to develop a growth mindset to achieve success in network marketing and MLM. Embrace challenges, learn from failures, and seek out opportunities for growth and development.

4. Stay focused

Distractions can derail your progress and hinder your success. To stay focused, prioritize your tasks, and stay committed to your goals. Avoid multitasking and eliminate distractions that can take your attention away from your goals.

5. Take action

Success requires action. Take consistent and deliberate action towards your goals. Be proactive and take responsibility for your success. Don't wait for opportunities to come to you; create them yourself.

In conclusion, creating a successful mindset is essential to achieving success in network marketing and MLM. It requires belief in yourself, setting realistic goals, developing a growth mindset, staying focused, and taking action. With the right mindset, you can overcome challenges, achieve your goals, and reach your full potential.

Building Your Network Marketing and MLM Business

Prospecting and recruiting

Prospecting and recruiting are essential elements of network marketing and MLM. They are the lifeblood of any successful business, and without them, your business will not grow. In this chapter, we will discuss the importance of prospecting and recruiting in network marketing and MLM, and how you can master these skills to take your business to the next level.

Prospecting is the process of finding potential customers or business partners for your network marketing or MLM business. It is the first step in building your network, and it requires a lot of effort and dedication. To prospect effectively, you need to have a clear understanding of your target market, their needs, and their preferences. You also need to have a good understanding of your product or service, and how it can benefit your prospects.

One of the most effective ways to prospect is through referrals. Referrals are people who have been referred to you by someone they trust. They are more likely to trust you and your business, and they are more likely to become customers or business partners. You can also prospect through social media, email marketing, and events.

Recruiting is the process of finding people who are interested in joining your network marketing or MLM business as business partners. It is a crucial step in building your network, and it requires a lot of effort and dedication. To recruit effectively, you need to have a clear understanding of your business, its benefits, and its compensation plan. You also need to have good communication skills, and the ability to motivate and inspire people.

One of the most effective ways to recruit is through personal contact. Talk to people you know, and ask them if they are interested in joining your business. You can also recruit through social media, events, and online marketing.

In conclusion, prospecting and recruiting are essential elements of network marketing and MLM. They require a lot of effort and dedication, but they are also the key to success. By mastering these skills, you can take your business to the next level and achieve your financial goals. So, start prospecting and recruiting today, and watch your network and your income grow.

Finding potential customers and team members

Finding potential customers and team members is a crucial aspect of achieving success in network marketing and MLM. In order to generate the kind of income that you desire, you need a large customer base and a strong team of individuals who are willing to work hard and help you build your business.

The first step in finding potential customers is to identify your target market. Consider the types of products or services that your company offers and think about who would be most interested in them. Once you have a clear idea of your target market, you can begin to develop a strategy for reaching out to potential customers.

One effective way to find potential customers is through social media. Platforms like Facebook, Instagram, and Twitter allow you to connect with people who are interested in your niche and engage with them directly. You can also use social media to promote your products and services and share valuable content that will help to build your brand and attract new customers.

Another effective way to find potential customers is through networking events and trade shows. These events provide an opportunity to meet with other business owners and networkers who may be interested in your products or services. Be sure to bring plenty of business cards and promotional materials to hand out at these events, and be prepared to engage in meaningful conversations that can help you build relationships with potential customers.

When it comes to finding potential team members, the key is to focus on recruiting individuals who share your values and vision for your business. Look for people who are motivated, hardworking, and passionate about your products and services. You can recruit team members through social media, networking events, and by reaching out to your existing network of contacts.

Overall, finding potential customers and team members is an ongoing process that requires patience, persistence, and a willingness to put in the work. By developing a clear strategy and utilizing a variety of tactics, you can build a strong customer base and team that will help you achieve your income goals in network marketing and MLM.

Approaching prospects

Approaching prospects is one of the most important steps in network marketing and MLM. It is the foundation of your business and the key to your success. Approaching prospects is not an easy task, but with the right mindset and skills, you can become a pro at it.

The first step in approaching prospects is to identify your ideal prospect. Who is your target audience? What are their needs and desires? What are their pain points? Once you have identified your ideal prospect, you can start creating a plan to approach them.

The second step is to build a relationship with your prospect. People do business with those they know, like, and trust. Take the time to get to know your prospect, listen to their needs, and offer them solutions to their problems. Show them that you genuinely care about their success and are willing to help them achieve their goals.

The third step is to present your business opportunity. Be clear and concise about what your business is all about, the benefits of joining your team, and what sets your business apart from others in the market. Use visual aids, such as a brochure or video presentation, to help your prospect understand the opportunity better.

The fourth step is to follow up with your prospect. Don't be afraid to follow up with your prospect after your initial presentation. Follow-up is crucial in network marketing and MLM, as it shows your prospect that you are serious about helping them achieve their goals. Be persistent but not pushy, and always offer value in your follow-up.

In conclusion, approaching prospects is an essential step in network marketing and MLM. It is the foundation of your business, and the key to your success. Remember to identify your ideal prospect, build a relationship with them, present your business opportunity, and follow up with them. With these skills, you can become a pro at approaching prospects and achieve your financial goals in network marketing and MLM.

Following up with prospects

Following up with prospects is one of the most important steps in network marketing and MLM. It's the process of keeping in touch with potential customers and clients who have shown interest in your business. Following up is crucial because it helps you build a relationship with your prospects, establish trust, and eventually close the sale. In this chapter, we'll share some tips and strategies on how to effectively follow up with your prospects.

1. Set a Follow-up Schedule

One of the best ways to ensure that you follow up with your prospects is to create a follow-up schedule. This schedule should include the date and time when you'll contact your prospects. You can use a calendar or a CRM software to keep track of your follow-up schedule. Having a schedule will help you stay organized and ensure that you don't miss any follow-ups.

2. Personalize Your Follow-up

When you follow up with your prospects, it's important to personalize your communication. Address your prospect by their name and use their specific interests or needs in your conversation. This shows that you care about them and their needs, and it also helps build rapport.

3. Provide Value

When following up with prospects, it's important to provide value. Share helpful tips, insights, and resources that can benefit your prospects. This not only shows that you're knowledgeable but also helps build trust and credibility.

4. Use Multiple Channels

Don't rely on just one communication channel to follow up with your prospects. Use multiple channels such as email, phone, social media, and even in-person meetings. This will increase the chances of reaching your prospects and help you build a stronger relationship with them.

5. Be Persistent

Following up with prospects requires persistence. Don't give up after just one or two attempts. Keep following up until you get a response. Remember, it takes time to build a relationship and close a sale.

In conclusion, following up with prospects is a critical step in network marketing and MLM. By setting a follow-up schedule, personalizing your communication, providing value, using multiple channels, and being persistent, you can effectively follow up with your prospects and increase your chances of closing the sale.

Building a team

Building a Team

One of the essential components of achieving success in network marketing and MLM is building a strong and effective team. A team that is committed, motivated, and focused on the same goals can make all the difference in your business. Here are some tips on how to build a winning team.

1. Define your vision: Your team needs to know what they are working towards. Clearly define your vision, mission, and goals for your network marketing and MLM business. Communicate these to your team, so everyone is on the same page.

2. Recruit effectively: Building a team requires recruiting the right people. Look for individuals who share your vision and values. They should be passionate, motivated, and willing to learn. Avoid recruiting people solely based on their network or social status.

3. Train and support: Once you have recruited your team, provide them with the necessary training and support. This will help them develop the skills they need to succeed in network marketing and MLM. Provide ongoing support to ensure they stay motivated and engaged.

4. Set goals and rewards: Set goals for your team and reward them for achieving them. This can be a great way to keep your team motivated and focused. Celebrate your team's successes and recognize their hard work.

5. Foster a positive culture: Building a team requires creating a positive culture. Encourage open communication, collaboration, and teamwork. Create

a supportive and encouraging environment where everyone feels valued and respected.

6. Lead by example: As a leader, you need to lead by example. Your team will look up to you and follow your lead. Be a positive role model, demonstrate the behaviors and values you want your team to emulate.

Building a strong and effective team takes time and effort. But with the right approach, you can create a team that is committed, motivated, and focused on achieving success in network marketing and MLM. Remember to define your vision, recruit effectively, train and support, set goals and rewards, foster a positive culture, and lead by example.

Training and supporting team members

Training and supporting team members is a crucial aspect of achieving success in network marketing and MLM. As a business owner or networker, it is essential to recognize that your team members are the backbone of your business. Therefore, investing in their training and supporting them is a vital step towards achieving your financial goals.

One of the best ways to train your team members is by organizing regular training sessions. These sessions can be conducted online or in-person and can cover various topics such as sales techniques, product knowledge, and customer service. By providing your team members with the necessary skills and knowledge, you can empower them to become more effective in their roles and contribute positively to your business's growth.

It is also important to provide ongoing support to your team members. This can be done by establishing open lines of communication and being available to answer their questions and address their concerns. By creating a supportive environment, you can foster a sense of teamwork, trust, and loyalty among your team members, which can ultimately lead to increased productivity and profitability for your business.

In addition to training and support, it is essential to recognize and reward your team members for their hard work and contributions. This can be done by offering incentives such as bonuses, promotions, and recognition for achieving specific goals or milestones. By acknowledging and rewarding your team members' efforts, you can motivate them to continue striving towards their goals and contribute positively to your business's success.

In conclusion, training and supporting team members is a critical aspect of achieving success in network marketing and MLM. By investing in your team members' training, providing ongoing support, and recognizing their contributions, you can create a positive and productive work environment that can lead to increased profitability and success for your business.

Motivating and incentivizing team members

Motivating and incentivizing team members is one of the most important things you can do as a network marketer or MLM professional. Your team is the backbone of your business, and if they are not motivated and engaged, your business will suffer. In this chapter, we will discuss some strategies that you can use to motivate and incentivize your team members.

First and foremost, it's important to understand that motivation is personal. What motivates one person may not motivate another. This is why it's essential to get to know your team members on a personal level. Take the time to understand their goals, aspirations, and what drives them. Once you understand what motivates them, you can tailor your approach to incentivizing and motivating them.

One strategy that has proven to be effective is recognition. People love to be recognized for their hard work and accomplishments. Make it a point to celebrate your team members' successes, whether it's a promotion, hitting a sales goal, or achieving a personal milestone. Recognition can be as simple as a shout-out in a team meeting or as elaborate as an awards ceremony.

Another effective strategy is to provide incentives. Incentives can come in many forms, including bonuses, trips, and gifts. The key is to make the incentive something that your team members truly desire. For example, if you know that one of your team members loves to travel, offer a trip as an incentive for hitting a sales goal. Or, if you know that another team member is saving up for a new car, offer a bonus that will help them get closer to their goal.

Training and development opportunities are also powerful motivators. People want to grow and develop in their careers, and providing them with training and development opportunities can help keep them engaged and motivated. This could include attending conferences, taking online courses, or participating in mentorship programs.

Finally, it's essential to lead by example. If you want your team members to be motivated and engaged, you need to model that behavior yourself. Be enthusiastic, positive, and engaged in your work. Show your team members that you care about their success and are invested in their growth.

In conclusion, motivating and incentivizing team members is critical to the success of your network marketing or MLM business. By understanding what motivates your team members, providing recognition and incentives, offering training and development opportunities, and leading by example, you can create a motivated and engaged team that will help you achieve your goals.

Handling team conflict

Handling Team Conflict

As a network marketer or MLM business owner, you are likely to face team conflict at some point. Conflict is inevitable in any business, and how you handle it can make a significant difference in your team's success.

The first step in handling team conflict is to identify the cause. Conflict can arise from various reasons, such as differences in personalities, goals, or work styles. Once you identify the cause, you can take the necessary steps to resolve the issue.

One effective approach to resolving team conflict is to encourage open communication. Encourage your team members to express their concerns and ideas openly. Listen carefully to each person's perspective and try to understand their point of view. This helps to build trust and respect among team members.

Another approach is to establish clear expectations and guidelines. Ensure that everyone understands their roles and responsibilities and the team's overall objective. This way, everyone is working towards the same goal, and there is less room for misunderstandings.

If the conflict persists, consider bringing in a neutral third party to mediate. This could be a professional mediator or someone from outside the team who can provide an unbiased perspective.

In some cases, conflict may be unavoidable, and you may need to make tough decisions. As a leader, you must be willing to make difficult decisions that are in the best interest of the team and the business. This may mean making changes to the team composition or redefining roles and responsibilities.

Remember, conflict is not always a bad thing. It can lead to new ideas, perspectives, and approaches. As a leader, your role is to manage conflict effectively and turn it into a positive force for growth and development.

In conclusion, handling team conflict is an essential skill for any network marketer or MLM business owner. By establishing clear expectations, encouraging open communication, and making tough decisions when necessary, you can resolve conflict and build a strong, successful team.

Marketing and promoting your business

Marketing and Promoting Your Business

Marketing and promoting your business is essential to the success of your network marketing and MLM business. Without effective marketing and promotion, your business will not reach its full potential. In this chapter, we will discuss some effective marketing and promotional strategies to help you grow your business and reach your goal of earning $10,000 per month.

1. Build a Strong Online Presence

In today's digital age, having a strong online presence is crucial. This includes having a professional website, social media accounts, and email marketing campaigns. Your website should be optimized for search engines, mobile-friendly, and have a compelling call-to-action. Your social media accounts should be active and engaging with your target audience. And your email marketing campaigns should provide value and promote your products or services.

2. Attend Networking Events

Networking events are a great way to meet new people and expand your network. Attend local business events, trade shows, and conferences related to your industry. Be sure to bring plenty of business cards and be ready to pitch your business. You never know who you may meet that could become a valuable business contact or customer.

3. Host Workshops and Webinars

Hosting workshops and webinars is an effective way to position yourself as an expert in your field and provide value to potential customers. Choose a topic related to your business and provide valuable information that attendees can use. Be sure to promote your workshop or webinar on your website, social media, and email marketing campaigns.

4. Utilize Referral Marketing

Referral marketing is one of the most effective forms of marketing. Encourage your existing customers to refer their friends and family to your business. Offer incentives for referrals such as discounts or free products. This can help you grow your customer base and increase sales.

5. Leverage Influencer Marketing

Influencer marketing is a powerful way to reach new customers. Identify influencers in your industry and reach out to them to promote your products or services. This can be done through sponsored posts, product reviews, or brand collaborations. Influencer marketing can help you reach a wider audience and increase brand awareness.

In conclusion, marketing and promoting your business is essential to the success of your network marketing and MLM business. Build a strong online presence, attend networking events, host workshops and webinars, utilize referral marketing, and leverage influencer marketing to help you reach your goal of earning $10,000 per month. By implementing these strategies, you can grow your business and achieve the success you desire.

Creating a personal brand

Creating a Personal Brand

Creating a personal brand is essential for anyone who wants to succeed in the world of network marketing and MLM. Your personal brand is what sets you apart from everyone else and establishes your unique identity. It is a reflection of your values, beliefs, and personality, and it helps people understand why they should do business with you.

To create a personal brand, you need to identify your unique selling proposition (USP). This is the one thing that sets you apart from everyone else in your industry. It could be your expertise, your experience, your personality, or your approach to business. Whatever it is, it needs to be something that your target audience values and that you can deliver consistently.

Once you have identified your USP, you need to develop a branding strategy. This includes creating a brand name, logo, tagline, and brand message that reflect your USP and appeal to your target audience. Your branding strategy should be consistent across all your marketing materials, including your website, social media profiles, business cards, and marketing materials.

Another important aspect of creating a personal brand is building your online presence. This includes establishing a strong presence on social media platforms like Facebook, Twitter, and LinkedIn, as well as creating a professional website that showcases your expertise and services. Your online presence should be a reflection of your personal brand and should reinforce your USP and brand message.

Finally, you need to establish yourself as an expert in your field. This means creating valuable content that showcases your expertise and sharing it with your target audience. You can do this through blog posts, articles, videos, and social media updates. By establishing yourself as an expert, you will build trust with your target audience and establish yourself as a go-to resource in your industry.

In conclusion, creating a personal brand is essential for anyone who wants to succeed in network marketing and MLM. By identifying your USP, developing a branding strategy, building your online presence, and establishing yourself as an expert, you can create a personal brand that sets you apart from everyone else and helps you achieve your business goals.

Utilizing social media

Utilizing Social Media

In today's digital age, social media has become an essential tool for businesses and marketers to reach out to their target audience. With its vast reach and engagement potential, social media platforms offer an affordable and effective way to promote your network marketing or MLM business.

One of the biggest advantages of social media is that it allows you to connect with people from all over the world. This means that you can expand your network beyond your local community and tap into a global market. By leveraging platforms like Facebook, Instagram, Twitter, LinkedIn, and YouTube, you can reach out to potential customers or business partners and build relationships with them.

However, it's not enough to simply create a social media account and start posting content. To make the most of your social media presence, you need to have a well-defined strategy. This involves identifying your target audience, creating compelling content, and engaging with your followers.

One way to engage with your audience is by hosting live videos or webinars, where you can share your knowledge and expertise about your products or services. This not only helps you build credibility and authority in your niche but also allows you to connect with potential customers on a personal level.

Another way to leverage social media is by using paid advertising. Platforms like Facebook and Instagram offer targeted advertising options that allow you to reach out to people based on their interests, demographics, and behaviors. By investing in paid advertising, you can increase your visibility and attract more leads to your business.

In addition to promoting your products or services, social media can also be used to build your personal brand. By sharing your story, values, and passions, you can attract like-minded people who resonate with your message. This can help you establish yourself as a thought leader in your industry and attract new business opportunities.

In conclusion, social media is a powerful tool that can help you take your network marketing or MLM business to the next level. By utilizing social media platforms effectively, you can expand your reach, build relationships, and attract more leads to your business.

Hosting events and presentations

Hosting events and presentations is an essential part of network marketing and MLM. It is a powerful way to attract potential customers, build relationships, and increase sales. In this subchapter, we will discuss the benefits of hosting events and presentations, how to plan and organize them, and some tips for making them successful.

Benefits of Hosting Events and Presentations

Hosting events and presentations can provide numerous benefits for your network marketing and MLM business. Here are some of the advantages:

1. Builds Credibility

Hosting events and presentations can help establish your business as an authority in the industry. It shows that you are knowledgeable about your products and services, and you are willing to share that knowledge with others.

2. Attracts Potential Customers

Events and presentations are an excellent way to attract potential customers. It gives them the opportunity to learn more about your products and services, and how they can benefit from them.

3. Builds Relationships

Hosting events and presentations can help you build relationships with your existing customers and potential customers. It provides a platform to interact with them, answer their questions, and address their concerns.

4. Increases Sales

Events and presentations can help increase sales by providing an opportunity for customers to make purchases, and by creating a sense of urgency to buy.

How to Plan and Organize Events and Presentations

Organizing events and presentations can be challenging, but with proper planning, it can be a success. Here are some steps to follow:

1. Define Your Goals

The first step is to define your goals. What do you want to achieve from the event or presentation? Is it to attract new customers, increase sales, or build relationships?

2. Choose a Venue

Choose a venue that can accommodate your audience, and that is easily accessible. Consider the location, parking, and amenities.

3. Create a Budget

Create a budget for the event or presentation. Consider the costs of the venue, speakers, marketing, and refreshments.

4. Choose a Theme

Choose a theme for the event or presentation. This can be based on your products or services, or a topic that is relevant to your audience.

5. Invite Speakers

Invite speakers who can provide value to your audience. They can be industry experts, business leaders, or successful network marketers.

6. Market the Event

Market the event or presentation through social media, email marketing, and word of mouth. Use attractive graphics and catchy headlines to attract potential attendees.

Tips for Making Events and Presentations Successful

Here are some tips for making your events and presentations successful:

1. Be Prepared

Be prepared for the event or presentation. Have all your materials ready, and rehearse your presentation beforehand.

2. Engage Your Audience

Engage your audience by asking questions, providing interactive activities, and encouraging participation.

3. Provide Value

Provide value to your audience by offering insights, tips, and strategies that they can use in their business or personal life.

4. Follow Up

Follow up with attendees after the event or presentation. Send them a thank you email, and provide them with additional information or resources.

In conclusion, hosting events and presentations can be a powerful way to attract potential customers, build relationships, and increase sales. By following the steps outlined in this subchapter, and applying the tips provided, you can make your events and presentations successful and beneficial for your network marketing and MLM business.

Maximizing Your Earnings Potential

Increasing sales volume

Increasing sales volume is a critical component of any network marketing or MLM business. Without sales, your business will not generate the revenue necessary to sustain itself and grow. Therefore, it is essential to have a solid plan in place to increase your sales volume.

One way to increase sales volume is by identifying your target audience. Who are the people that are most likely to be interested in your product or service? Once you have identified your ideal customer, you can tailor your marketing efforts to appeal to them specifically. This could involve creating targeted ads, developing targeted social media content, or even hosting events that cater to their interests.

Another effective strategy for increasing sales volume is by creating a sense of urgency. This can be achieved by offering limited-time promotions or discounts to your customers. This will incentivize them to make a purchase sooner rather than later, which can help boost your sales volume.

You can also increase sales volume by offering incentives to your customers. This could be in the form of loyalty programs, referral bonuses, or even free gifts with purchase. By offering these incentives, you are encouraging your customers to continue doing business with you and referring others to your business.

Lastly, it is important to constantly evaluate and adjust your sales strategies. What is working for your business, and what is not? By regularly reviewing your sales data and adjusting your approach as needed, you can continue to optimize your sales volume and achieve even greater success.

In conclusion, increasing sales volume is crucial for the success of any network marketing or MLM business. By identifying your target audience, creating a sense of urgency, offering incentives, and constantly evaluating and adjusting your sales strategies, you can increase your sales volume and achieve your financial goals.

Utilizing product knowledge

Utilizing Product Knowledge

One of the most important aspects of succeeding in network marketing and MLM is having an in-depth knowledge of the products you are promoting. This is because your product knowledge can make or break your business, and can be the difference between making a sale or not.

Product knowledge refers to understanding the features, benefits, and value of your products. This knowledge is essential because it helps you to communicate effectively with your prospects and customers, and also helps you to build trust and credibility.

To utilize product knowledge, you need to start by understanding the benefits of your products. What problems do they solve? What needs do they meet? How do they make people's lives better? Once you know the answers to these questions, you can easily explain to your prospects how your products can benefit them.

Another important aspect of product knowledge is knowing the ingredients or materials used to make the products. This will help you to answer any questions your prospects may have about the product and also help you to highlight the unique features and benefits of your products.

In addition, you need to know the price of your products and how they compare to other products in the market. This will help you to determine the best selling points for your products and also help you to convince your prospects that your products are worth the price.

Utilizing product knowledge can also help you to identify your target market. By understanding the benefits and features of your products, you can easily identify the people who are most likely to buy them. This will help you to focus your marketing efforts on the right people and also help you to increase your sales.

In conclusion, product knowledge is a critical component of network marketing and MLM success. Without it, you will struggle to convince your prospects to buy your products and build a loyal customer base. Therefore, take the time to learn everything you can about your products, and use this knowledge to build your business and achieve your financial goals.

Cross-selling and upselling

Cross-selling and upselling are two crucial marketing strategies that can help you increase your sales and revenue in network marketing and MLM. While cross-selling refers to offering additional products or services to customers who have already made a purchase, upselling involves convincing customers to upgrade or purchase a higher-priced item.

One of the most significant benefits of cross-selling and upselling is that they can help you build stronger relationships with your customers. By offering them additional products or services that complement their previous purchases, you can show them that you understand their needs and are committed to providing them with the best possible experience.

To succeed in cross-selling and upselling, you need to have a deep understanding of your customers' needs and preferences. By analyzing their purchase history and behavior, you can identify the products or services that they are most likely to be interested in and tailor your offers accordingly.

Another key factor in effective cross-selling and upselling is creating a sense of urgency or scarcity. By highlighting the benefits of your offers and emphasizing that they are only available for a limited time, you can encourage customers to act quickly and make a purchase.

In addition to boosting your sales and revenue, cross-selling and upselling can also help you increase customer loyalty and retention. By providing your customers with a comprehensive range of products or services that meet their needs, you can establish yourself as a trusted and reliable provider and encourage them to continue doing business with you.

In conclusion, cross-selling and upselling are powerful marketing strategies that can help you achieve your goal of earning $10,000 per month through network marketing and MLM. By understanding your customers' needs, offering them targeted and compelling offers, and creating a sense of urgency, you can increase your sales, build stronger relationships, and establish yourself as a leader in your industry.

Providing excellent customer service

Providing excellent customer service is a crucial aspect of any successful business, including network marketing and MLM. It is essential to remember that customers are the lifeblood of any business, and without them, there would be no business at all. Therefore, it is essential to provide excellent customer service to retain existing customers and attract new ones.

To provide excellent customer service, you need to understand what your customers need and want. You need to listen to their concerns, answer their questions promptly, and go the extra mile to ensure they are satisfied with your products or services. Remember, happy customers are more likely to refer your business to others, which can help you grow your network marketing and MLM business.

Another essential aspect of providing excellent customer service is to be available when your customers need you. You should always be reachable via phone, email, or social media to answer any questions or concerns your customers may have. If you are unable to respond immediately, make sure to acknowledge their message and let them know when you will be able to get back to them.

In addition to being available and attentive, it is also crucial to be honest and transparent with your customers. If there is an issue with your product or service, be upfront about it and work with your customers to find a solution. Honesty and transparency will help build trust with your customers, which is essential for long-term success in network marketing and MLM.

Finally, make sure to follow up with your customers regularly. Check in with them to see how they are enjoying your products or services and if there is anything else you can do to improve their experience. Following up shows that you care about your customers and are committed to providing excellent customer service.

In conclusion, providing excellent customer service is essential for success in network marketing and MLM. By understanding your customers' needs, being available, honest, transparent, and following up regularly, you can build strong relationships with your customers and grow your business.

Advancing in rank and leadership

Advancing in rank and leadership is one of the key elements of success in network marketing and MLM. As you grow and develop your skills, you can increase your influence and impact, which can lead to greater income and success. In this chapter, we will explore some of the strategies and tools you can use to advance in rank and become a more effective leader in your network marketing business.

The first step towards advancing in rank is to focus on your personal development. This means investing time and effort in learning new skills, developing your mindset, and building your confidence. By becoming a better version of yourself, you will be better equipped to lead and inspire others.

Another important strategy for advancing in rank is to build strong relationships with your team members. This involves listening to their needs and concerns, providing support and encouragement, and helping them to develop their own skills and abilities. By building strong relationships with your team, you can create a culture of mutual respect and trust, which can help to drive success and growth throughout your network marketing business.

In addition to personal development and relationship-building, there are also a number of practical strategies you can use to advance in rank and leadership. These might include setting clear goals and targets, developing a strong work ethic, and leveraging technology and social media to connect with new prospects and customers.

Ultimately, advancing in rank and leadership in network marketing requires a combination of skills, strategies, and mindset. By focusing on your personal development, building strong relationships with your team, and using practical strategies to drive growth and success, you can become a more effective leader and reach your goals of earning $10,000 or more per month through network marketing and MLM.

Meeting and exceeding goals

Meeting and exceeding goals is an essential aspect of achieving success in network marketing and MLM. Setting goals and developing a plan to achieve them is the first step in the journey towards achieving financial freedom and independence. However, it takes more than just setting goals to ensure success. You must be willing to put in the work required and make the necessary sacrifices to reach your objectives.

To begin with, you need to have a clear understanding of what you want to achieve. Define your goals in terms of income, rank advancement, or the number of people you want to recruit into your team. Be specific and set a deadline for achieving each of your goals. This will help you to stay focused and motivated, even when the going gets tough.

The next step is to develop a plan of action. Break down your goals into smaller, more manageable tasks that you can accomplish on a daily, weekly, or monthly basis. Create a to-do list for each day and prioritize your tasks based on their importance and urgency. Regularly review your progress and make adjustments to your plan as needed.

One of the keys to meeting and exceeding your goals is to consistently take action. Don't wait for the perfect moment or opportunity to present itself before you take action. Instead, take action now and adjust your course as you go along. Remember, progress is better than perfection.

Another important factor in achieving your goals is to surround yourself with people who support and encourage you. Join a mastermind group, attend network marketing events, and connect with other successful network marketers and MLM professionals. This will give you the motivation and inspiration you need to keep going, even when the going gets tough.

Finally, celebrate your successes along the way. Give yourself a pat on the back for a job well done, no matter how small the accomplishment. This will help you to stay motivated and focused on achieving your ultimate goal of financial freedom and independence.

In conclusion, meeting and exceeding your goals in network marketing and MLM requires a combination of goal setting, planning, taking action, surrounding yourself with supportive people, and celebrating your successes. By following these guidelines, you can achieve your financial goals and build a successful network marketing and MLM business.

Developing leadership skills

Developing leadership skills is essential for anyone who wants to succeed in network marketing and MLM. Whether you are a business owner, employee, or self-employed, having strong leadership skills can help you to build a successful team and achieve your goals.

The first step in developing leadership skills is to understand what it means to be a leader. A leader is someone who inspires and motivates their team to work towards a common goal. They are able to communicate effectively, delegate tasks, and make decisions that benefit the team as a whole.

To become a leader in network marketing and MLM, it is important to focus on personal development. This means taking the time to learn new skills, improve your communication abilities, and develop your emotional intelligence. You should also work on building your confidence and self-esteem, as these traits are essential for effective leadership.

Another important aspect of developing leadership skills is to lead by example. This means practicing what you preach and setting a positive example for your team to follow. You should be willing to roll up your sleeves and work alongside your team to achieve your goals.

Effective leadership also involves being able to delegate tasks and responsibilities to others. This means trusting your team members to take on important tasks and empowering them to make decisions on their own. By doing this, you can build a strong team that is capable of achieving great things.

In summary, developing leadership skills is essential for anyone who wants to succeed in network marketing and MLM. By focusing on personal development, leading by example, and delegating tasks and responsibilities, you can become a strong and effective leader who inspires and motivates your team to achieve their goals.

Leading by example

Leading by example is an essential aspect of network marketing and MLM success. When you lead by example, you inspire others to follow in your footsteps and achieve their own success. However, leading by example is easier said than done. It requires a lot of hard work, dedication, and perseverance.

To lead by example, you need to set a high standard for yourself. You must be willing to put in the time and effort required to achieve your goals. You must also be willing to take risks and try new things. When you lead by example, you show others that anything is possible if they are willing to work hard and stay committed.

One of the best ways to lead by example is to be a great listener. When you listen to others, you show them that you care about their needs and are willing to help them achieve their goals. You also gain valuable insights into their needs and desires, which can help you tailor your approach to better meet their needs.

Another important aspect of leading by example is to be a great communicator. When you communicate effectively, you can convey your message clearly and inspire others to take action. You must also be able to listen to others and respond to their concerns and questions.

Leading by example also requires a strong work ethic. You must be willing to put in the time and effort required to achieve your goals. You must also be willing to learn and grow as a person and as a business owner. When you lead by example, you inspire others to do the same.

In conclusion, leading by example is an essential part of network marketing and MLM success. When you lead by example, you inspire others to achieve their own success. To lead by example, you must set a high standard for yourself, be a great listener and communicator, have a strong work ethic, and be willing to learn and grow. With these qualities, you can achieve great success in network marketing and MLM.

Diversifying income streams

Diversifying Income Streams

One of the biggest advantages of network marketing and MLM is the ability to diversify your income streams. This means having multiple sources of income coming in from various products or services that you offer.

Diversifying your income streams is essential to building a strong and sustainable business. It helps to reduce your risk and provides a safety net if one of your income streams dries up.

Here are some ways to diversify your income streams in network marketing and MLM:

1. Offer a variety of products or services: If you only have one product or service, you are limiting your income potential. Consider adding additional products or services that complement your existing offerings.

2. Develop multiple sales channels: Don't rely solely on one sales channel such as your website or social media. Explore other sales channels such as email marketing, direct mail, or even in-person events.

3. Create multiple income streams within your business: Consider creating a membership program, offering coaching services, or selling digital products such as eBooks or courses.

4. Partner with other businesses: Partnering with other businesses can help you reach a wider audience and offer additional products or services to your customers.

5. Build a team: Building a team of like-minded individuals who share your vision can help you leverage their skills and strengths to create additional income streams.

Remember, diversifying your income streams takes time and effort. It requires you to continually evaluate your business and look for new opportunities. But the rewards can be significant, providing you with a more stable and profitable business in the long run.

In conclusion, diversifying your income streams is a crucial component of building a successful network marketing and MLM business. It allows you to maximize your income potential, reduce risk, and create a more sustainable business. By implementing these strategies, you can create a strong foundation for your business and achieve your financial goals.

Exploring other network marketing opportunities

Exploring Other Network Marketing Opportunities

If you've been in the network marketing industry for quite some time, you might have already exhausted all the opportunities within your current company. But don't worry, there's a whole world of network marketing out there waiting for you to explore.

Before you jump into a new opportunity, it's important to do your research. Here are some tips to help you find the right opportunity for you:

1. Look for a company with a proven track record. Find out how long they've been in business, and check their financial stability. You want to make sure you're investing your time and money into a company that's going to be around for the long haul.

2. Check the compensation plan. Make sure it's fair and that you can make a decent income from it. Look for a plan that rewards both your personal sales and your team's sales.

3. Research the products. Are they high quality? Do they appeal to a wide audience? Are they something you'd be proud to represent?

4. Look for a supportive team. Find out if the company offers training and support to help you grow your business. You want to work with a team that's going to help you succeed.

5. Trust your gut. If something doesn't feel right, it probably isn't. Don't be afraid to walk away from an opportunity if it doesn't align with your values or goals.

Remember, network marketing is all about building relationships. You want to work with a company that values its customers and distributors, and that's committed to helping you succeed.

So, where can you find other network marketing opportunities? Here are some ideas:

1. Attend industry events. Network with other distributors and learn about new companies and products.

2. Use social media. Join online groups and communities to connect with other network marketers and learn about new opportunities.

3. Ask your friends and family. If you have friends or family members who are in network marketing, ask them for recommendations.

4. Use search engines. Do a search for "network marketing companies" or "MLM opportunities" to find new companies to explore.

Remember, there's no one-size-fits-all solution when it comes to network marketing. You need to find the opportunity that's right for you and your goals. By doing your research and trusting your instincts, you can find the perfect opportunity to help you achieve your financial dreams.

Creating additional income streams

Creating Additional Income Streams

One of the biggest advantages of network marketing and MLM is the ability to create multiple streams of income. This means that you can earn money from more than one source, which can help you achieve your financial goals faster. Here are some tips on how to create additional income streams:

1. Diversify your product offerings

If you're currently selling one product, consider adding more products to your line. This will allow you to appeal to a wider audience and increase your sales. For example, if you're selling health supplements, you could also offer skincare products or weight loss programs.

2. Expand your customer base

One way to increase your income is to expand your customer base. This can be done by attending events, networking with other professionals in your industry, and leveraging social media platforms to reach a wider audience.

3. Create digital products

Digital products, such as e-books, courses, and webinars, can be a great way to generate additional income. These products can be created once and sold multiple times, providing a passive income stream.

4. Offer services

If you have a skill or expertise, consider offering services to others. For example, if you're a graphic designer, you could offer design services to businesses. This can be a great way to earn additional income while also building your personal brand.

5. Invest in real estate

Real estate can be a great way to generate passive income. Consider investing in rental properties or house flipping to create an additional income stream.

By creating multiple streams of income, you can diversify your revenue streams and reduce your reliance on one source of income. This can help you achieve your financial goals faster and provide greater stability in your financial situation.

Overcoming Challenges and Obstacles

Dealing with rejection and negativity

Dealing with rejection and negativity is a critical aspect of network marketing and MLM. It is inevitable that you will encounter people who are not interested in what you have to offer or who will reject your proposals outright. While this can be discouraging, it is essential to remember that rejection is not necessarily a reflection of your abilities or worthiness. In fact, it is often a sign that you are putting yourself out there and taking risks.

One of the most important things you can do when dealing with rejection is to maintain a positive attitude. It is easy to become discouraged and negative when faced with rejection, but this will only serve to bring you down further. Instead, focus on the positives and keep your eye on the prize. Remember why you got into network marketing in the first place and keep that motivation in mind.

Another key strategy for dealing with rejection is to learn from it. Every rejection is an opportunity to improve your approach and refine your marketing strategies. Ask for feedback from those who reject you and take their comments on board. Use this feedback to make changes and improvements to your approach, and you may find that you start to see more success.

It is also important to remember that rejection is not personal. It is not a reflection of your worth or abilities. Everyone experiences rejection at some point in their lives, and it is a natural part of the process of putting yourself out there. Don't take it personally, and don't let it define you.

Finally, surround yourself with positive people who support you and believe in what you are doing. This can be especially important when you are dealing with rejection and negativity. Having a strong support system can help you stay motivated and focused, even when things are challenging.

In conclusion, dealing with rejection and negativity is an essential part of network marketing and MLM. It is important to maintain a positive attitude, learn from rejection, remember that it is not personal, and surround yourself with supportive people. By doing these things, you can stay motivated and focused on your goals, even in the face of rejection and negativity.

Balancing your business and personal life

Balancing Your Business and Personal Life

As an adult, business owner, parent, employee, employer, self-employed individual, networker, marketer, marketing manager, entertainer, start-up, or retiree, you have a plethora of responsibilities that require your attention. It can be challenging to balance your business and personal life, but it is imperative to maintain a healthy work-life balance to avoid burnout and maximize productivity.

Here are some tips to help you balance your business and personal life:

1. Create a Schedule: Set specific working hours and stick to them. When you are not working, focus on your personal life. This will help you avoid overworking and ensure that you have time for your loved ones.

2. Prioritize Your Tasks: Identify the most important tasks that need to be completed and focus on them first. This will help you accomplish your goals and reduce stress.

3. Delegate Tasks: It is essential to delegate tasks to others when you are overwhelmed with work. Delegating will help you focus on the most critical tasks and make the best use of your time.

4. Take Breaks: Taking regular breaks throughout the day can help you recharge and refocus. It is essential to take a break from work and spend time doing activities that you enjoy.

5. Work Out: Exercise is a great way to reduce stress and improve your overall health. Incorporate regular physical activity into your daily routine to maintain a healthy work-life balance.

6. Limit Distractions: Social media, emails, and phone calls can be a significant distraction during work hours. Turn off notifications or limit them during working hours to avoid distractions and stay focused.

7. Set Boundaries: Establish clear boundaries between your work and personal life. Avoid working during family time or personal activities and make sure to communicate your boundaries with your colleagues and loved ones.

Balancing your business and personal life can be challenging, but it is essential to maintain a healthy work-life balance to avoid burnout and maximize productivity. Incorporate these tips into your daily routine to achieve a balanced and fulfilling life.

Overcoming self-doubt and limiting beliefs

Overcoming self-doubt and limiting beliefs is a crucial step towards achieving success in any network marketing or MLM business. Often, we hold ourselves back from reaching our full potential due to negative thoughts and beliefs about ourselves.

To overcome self-doubt, it is important to first identify the root cause of the doubt. Is it a fear of failure or a lack of confidence in your abilities? Once you have identified the source, you can begin to work on overcoming it.

One effective method is to focus on your strengths and accomplishments. Make a list of all the things you have achieved in your life and the skills you possess. Remind yourself of your past successes and use them as motivation to push forward.

Another way to overcome self-doubt is to surround yourself with positive and supportive people. Seek out mentors or join a mastermind group where you can connect with like-minded individuals who can provide encouragement and guidance.

Limiting beliefs can also hold us back from achieving success in network marketing or MLM. These beliefs can be ingrained in our subconscious and can stem from past experiences, societal norms, or cultural conditioning.

To overcome limiting beliefs, it is important to challenge them and replace them with positive affirmations. For example, if you believe that you are not good at sales, challenge that belief by focusing on your strengths in building relationships and providing value to your customers.

It is also important to visualize yourself achieving success and to believe that it is possible. By visualizing your goals and believing in yourself, you can overcome any limiting beliefs that may be holding you back.

In conclusion, overcoming self-doubt and limiting beliefs is essential for success in network marketing and MLM. By identifying the root causes of these negative thoughts and beliefs, focusing on your strengths, surrounding yourself with positive people, challenging limiting beliefs, and visualizing success, you can achieve your goals and reach your full potential.

Conclusion

Recap of key points

Recap of Key Points

Congratulations! You've made it to the end of the book! We hope you've found the information useful and informative. Before we wrap up, let's recap some of the key points we've covered in this book.

First and foremost, we've emphasized the importance of mindset. Developing a positive, can-do attitude is essential for success in any endeavor, but particularly in network marketing and MLM. You need to believe in yourself, your products, and your company in order to inspire others to join you on your journey.

Secondly, we've discussed the importance of choosing the right company to work with. You want to work with a company that has a strong reputation, a solid product line, and a compensation plan that rewards your hard work. Do your due diligence and research potential companies before signing on the dotted line.

Thirdly, we've talked about the importance of building relationships. Network marketing and MLM are all about forming connections with others, whether it's through social media, face-to-face meetings, or events. Building trust and rapport with others is key to growing your business and achieving the success you desire.

Fourthly, we've discussed the importance of personal development. Investing in yourself through books, courses, and coaching can help you develop the skills and knowledge you need to excel in network marketing and MLM. Don't be afraid to invest in yourself and your business.

Finally, we've talked about the importance of taking action. All the knowledge and planning in the world won't get you anywhere if you don't take action. Set goals, make a plan, and take consistent action towards achieving those goals.

In conclusion, network marketing and MLM can be a lucrative and rewarding business opportunity for those who are willing to put in the work. By developing the right mindset, choosing the right company, building relationships, investing in personal development, and taking action, you can achieve your goal of earning $10,000 per month through network marketing and MLM. Good luck on your journey!

Final thoughts and encouragement

As we come to the end of this book, I want to take a moment to offer some final thoughts and encouragement to all of you who have read through and absorbed the ideas and strategies presented here. Whether you are an adult, business owner, parent, employee, employer, self-employed, networker, marketer, marketing manager, entertainer, start-up, or retired, you have taken an important step towards achieving your financial goals and building a successful network marketing or MLM business.

First and foremost, I want to emphasize that success in this field is not a matter of luck or talent alone. It requires hard work, dedication, persistence, and a willingness to learn and adapt to new challenges and opportunities. It also requires a clear understanding of what you want to achieve, why it matters to you, and how you plan to get there.

If you haven't already done so, I encourage you to take some time to reflect on your personal and professional goals, and to identify the specific steps you need to take to achieve them. This may involve setting specific targets for your income, your customer base, or your team size, as well as developing a detailed action plan to achieve those targets.

At the same time, I want to remind you that success in network marketing and MLM is not just about achieving your own goals. It is also about helping others to achieve theirs. As you build your business and your team, remember to focus on serving the needs of your customers and your downline, and to provide them with the guidance, support, and encouragement they need to succeed.

Finally, I want to encourage you to stay committed to your goals and to your vision for your business. There will be setbacks and challenges along the way, but if you remain focused and persistent, you can overcome them and achieve the success you desire.

Thank you for taking the time to read this book, and I wish you all the best of luck in your network marketing and MLM journey. Remember, with the right mindset, the right strategies, and the right support, you can go from zero to $10,000 monthly and beyond!

Call to action for readers to take the next steps in their network marketing and MLM journey.

Congratulations! You have made it this far in your network marketing and MLM journey. You have learned the basics, the strategies, the techniques, and the mindset to succeed in this industry. You have read this book, which means you are serious about taking your business to the next level.

Now, it's time to take action. You can't just read this book and expect miracles to happen. You have to implement what you have learned. You have to practice what you preach. You have to walk the talk. You have to hustle and grind.

Here are some call-to-action steps for you to take:

1. Set your goals - What do you want to achieve in your network marketing and MLM business? How much do you want to earn? How many people do you want to recruit? How many products do you want to sell? Write them down and make them specific, measurable, achievable, relevant, and time-bound.

2. Create your action plan - What are the steps you need to take to achieve your goals? What are the activities you need to do daily, weekly, monthly? What are the resources you need to invest in? What are the challenges you need to overcome? Write them down and make them actionable, realistic, and accountable.

3. Implement your action plan - What are you waiting for? Start doing what you need to do to achieve your goals. Don't procrastinate. Don't make excuses. Don't wait for the perfect moment. Just do it. Take massive action. Be consistent. Be persistent. Be disciplined.

4. Track your progress - How are you doing so far? Are you on track? Are you making progress? Are you achieving your goals? Use metrics, tools, and systems to track your performance. Analyze your results. Adjust your action plan if necessary. Learn from your mistakes. Celebrate your successes.

5. Share your story - How can you inspire others with your success story? How can you encourage others to join your team? How can you help others achieve their goals? Share your journey, your struggles, your lessons, and your triumphs. Be authentic. Be honest. Be generous.

Remember, success in network marketing and MLM is not a destination, it's a journey. It's not a one-time event, it's a continuous process. It's not a solo effort, it's a team effort. It's not a quick fix, it's a long-term commitment. It's not a magic formula, it's a combination of hard work, smart work, and heart work.

So, are you ready to take the next steps in your network marketing and MLM journey? Are you ready to turn your dreams into reality? Are you ready to make a difference in your life and the lives of others? If yes, then let's go!